YOGA for ROWERS

by Chrys Kozak

Yoga for Rowers

Copyright © 2009 by Chrys Kozak

www.YogaForRowers.com

All rights reserved. Printed in the United States of America. No part of this book may be used or reproduced in any manner whatsoever without written permission from the publisher. For information, address Chrys Kozak, 19537 Lake Road, Cleveland, Ohio 44116.

First printing: December 2009

FIRST EDITION

Designed by Chrys Kozak

Warning and Disclaimer

Every effort has been made to make this book as complete and accurate as possible, but no warranty or fitness is implied. The *Yoga for Rowers* program is intended for healthy adults. The information provided is on an "as is" basis and is solely for informational and educational purposes and is not medical advice. Always consult your doctor before starting any new fitness program or if you have questions about your health. Although every precaution has been taken in the preparation of this book, the publisher and author assume no responsibility for errors or omissions. Neither is any liability nor responsiblity assumed to any person or entity with respect to any loss or damages, personal or otherwise, arising from the information contained in this book.

Book Sales

This book is available at special discounts for bulk purchases, fundraisers, affiliates, and also educational, business or sales promotional use. For information please contact the author: *ChrysKozak@YogaForRowers.com.*

ISBN:1450546935

Manufactured in the United States of America

To Dad

FOCUS, BALANCE, FLEXIBILITY, POWER, STRENGTH

Table of **Contents**

I. Introduction: **Why yoga?**

II. Testimonials: **Yoga is the difference**

III. The Recovery: **Balance**

IV. The Catch: **Connection**

V. The Drive: **Power**

VI. The Finish: **Control**

VII. Workouts: **Prepare to succeed**

VIII. Conclusion: **Ohm your way to gold!**

Why yoga?

The rowers I've known in my life are a unique breed. They don't just lace up some shoes and go for a run or climb on an elliptical at the gym and call that a workout. These individuals are hardcore, intense competitors. In one of the most physically and mentally demanding sports there is, they will push themselves to their absolute limits just to get their boat across the finish line first.

It's a unique bond rowers share, regardless of where on the learning curve you are in the sport. True, there is the love of being on the water and feeling the boat glide poetically beneath you, leaving silent footprints in your wake as a nod to the gods you were here for a moment. But for competitors around the world, the bond goes one step farther. There is no Plan B, no tolerance for pain, and absolutely no excuses. There is only 100% complete commitment. And for those athletes who are up for the challenge, there is an unspoken respect for your sacrifice and dedication.

At first glance the idea of introducing yoga into a training program seems unusual. Chirping birds, ohming bowls, lots of breathing and twisting into a praying mantis - this is what my friends thought when I told them about a yoga plan designed specifically for rowers.

What a waste of time was the comment most often heard. We'd rather be erging, that's what makes us fast. I'm young and strong, I don't need it - or - I'm a masters rower, I've never done yoga so why start now? We want POWER, not meditation and Bhuddist philosophy. We'll lose our edge.

For athletes who are looking to achieve their peak mental & physical performance, whether you're a high school novice or a masters world champion, yoga IS the answer. It will give you the edge.

why yoga?

What you can expect from this book:

- Gain inches on your stroke (yes, I said inches!) by adding increased flexibility and a larger range of joint mobility
- Develop an obscene amount of power in your drive
- Strengthen your core and posture in record time
- Learn how to calm your mind by connecting with your breath, regardless if there are oars clashing or what your competitors are doing in the boat next to you
- Focus with laserlike concentration during practices and races
- Balance & maintain the boat's set no matter what the weather or boat conditions
- Have fewer injuries and quicker recovery time
- For younger rowers, yoga improves concentration
- For masters rowers, yoga increases the length of not only your stroke, but more importantly, the length of your rowing career

In races that are won by tenths of seconds and you're looking to squeeze every possible inch out of your stroke, YOGA IS THE DEFINITIVE EDGE.

Rowing is an unusual alchemy of blending power and grace.

Throw away the notion that yoga is a bunch of hippies on rubberized mats chanting in a fog of incense. ***Yoga is more like rowing than you might think.*** For centuries people have gracefully practiced fierce warrior poses dedicated to the gods. Practicing power and grace on the mat WILL transfer to power and grace in your boat. And you don't have to trade in your JL wardrobe for hemp clothing or become a vegan either. Thankfully, the traditional Guinness after practice can still be a staple in your diet.

Read this book and try the program. This is literally a down and dirty guide that breaks the stroke cycle into 4 phases and assigns 3 yoga poses per phase. Don't be deceived by the simplicity of the program - these poses pack a powerhouse! Power is not just sheer force in the boat, it's the ability to perform effectively. The poses in this book are targeted specifically for rowers to help them maximize their effectiveness on the water. Master these 12 poses and there is NO LIMIT to how well you perform this season!

Feel free to pick and choose which poses look interesting to you and which ones you want to start with - but remember the ones you find challenging should deserve extra attention. For example, if the seated forward bend causes you grief, chances are your hamstrings are tight. Practicing this pose, while potentially frustrating at first, will soon become easier as your flexibility is increased. All it takes for the *Yoga for Rowers* program to work is a very small time commitment and an open mind.

Commit to 3-4 times a week. Just start with 15-20 minutes. Do this and you will notice a definite difference in your split times and how the boat is moving.

That's honestly all it will take. You're only hours away from a longer stroke, more power, better concentration, a stronger team, more medals, less pain and injuries....and dare I say it, even a happier life.

Namaste rowers!

why yoga?

TESTIMONIALS

paul westbury: former new zealand olympic coach

You will be amazed how in 20 years of coaching rowing, yoga, breathing and anxiet control have been the catalyst for athletes to achieve their potential and, together with the on-the-water training, surpass goals beyond their wildest dreams.

Several examples include:

- Silver medal World Championships Finland 1995 NZL Men 4+
- Course record NZL 4+ Copenhagen 1995 6.01.28
- Mens Premier Eight NZ National Champions 2000
- Gozillion High School Naitonal Women Championship crews

aaron marcovy: 2008 oxford boat race champion, vesper rower, head of the charles competitor & us national team training camp

While training in Philadelphia, I was introduced to the benefits of yoga for rowers. We would practice yoga as a team weekly, in preparation for national competition and international event trials. For me, I found it helps to improve flexibility, circulation, balance, and concentration. I have introduced elements of yoga to the stretching and weight training regimen followed by all of the teams I now coach. Chrys Kozak's training methods are easily implemented, profoundly beneficial, and directly practical for sweep and scull oarspeople anywhere.

brad whitehead: harvard oarsman, 2009 us nationals bronze medalist sculler, 1st place 2009 chicago sprints & gold medalist at canadian henley

Rowing is 40% physical conditioning, 40% technique, and 50% mental toughness -- yoga can bring the flexibility to increase the intensity of training with less risk of injury and to achieve the form to go fast; even more importantly, it can brings the concentration and calm required to excel in the heat of competition.

yoga is the difference

tim denihan: head of the charles competitor, gold at fisa worlds, gold at us nationals

I used to just practice yoga in the off season when it was too cold to row. It was just something to keep my flexibility and muscles moving. Since I started adding yoga into my daily workouts - a few poses before going on the water and a few poses after - I can't believe the difference it's made. Being able to concentrate in a practice and do the drills with the same mental focas as you would have in a race is always difficult, especially when you know how much work you have to do at the office in a few hours. Yoga calms my mind so I can easily get into race-mentality during our daily practices. This has helped so much. My practices are more intense, the rowing is better and when we go to race, my whole boat knows we're unbeatable because we have the mental stamina to beat anyone.

jim kozak: rower, coach, head of the charles competitor, with over 50 gold medals

For the Masters rower, flexibility becomes increasingly important. As a 28 year old rower, I'm primarily concerned with speed and power. This book provides information on how to maximize both. This book shows you precise yoga poses that target a rower's most important muscle groups. The poses in this book are also focused on building strength that you're able to translate into acceleration and power in the drive.

matt previts: coxswain, hocr competitor & st. ignatius high school head rowing coach

Rowing requires a very high level of aerobic fitness, raw power, athletic balance, and mental toughness. The "secret ingredient" in this complex mixture is flexibility and focus. These two skills are developed and sharpened through consistent yoga practice. My oarsmen are more limber and agile once they have spent time doing yoga as part of their training regimen

paul kopp: masters rower & head of the charles competitor

I'm an individual who since high school graduation more the 30 years ago has immersed myself in competitive rowing. Through it all, I have found yoga and stretching to be the cornerstone of my training. These activities have helped me push beyond my norm by increasing my flexibility and allowing me to recover quickly between work-outs and from injuries. I believe yoga and stretching have definitely given me the ability to consistently perform at my peak potential for over 3 decades.

Yoga has a cult following in professional sports:

- Pro golfers Fred Couples, Annika Sorenstam and David Duval; NBA power houses Kevin Garnett, Shaquille O'Neal and Kareem Abdul-Jabar; football legend Dan Marino; track and field Olympian Carl Lewis; hockey star Mark Messier; baseball great Barry Bonds; racecar driver Danica Patrick; tennis stars Pete Sampras, Venus and Serena Williams; NBA coach Pat Riley; boxing champion Evander Holyfield...all yogis.

- Will Green of the Cleveland Browns practices yoga because it makes him more flexible, which gives him the advantage of more speed on the field.

- Tony Parrish of the San Francisco 49ers is a yoga advocate. After breaking his left ankle and fibula, he practiced yoga to get back into the game fast.

- Chauncy Billups, of the Detroit Pistons and MVP of the NBA Champions, does yoga mostly for mental reasons and to learn how to relax. He thinks it's great when your body is able to reach such a different level of relaxation in just a few minutes.

- Daylan Childress, pitcher for the Cincinnati Reds, gets on the mat because yoga relieves his body of all the stress he puts it through.

- Zen master Phil Jackson had his winning Bulls and Lakers teams doing team yoga workouts.

- Andrew Ethier from the Dogers practices yoga to keep him relaxed and focused in tense games.

these are some of the countless athletes who have adopted yoga as part of their training to achieve excellence in their sport and reduce both injuries and recovery time. they have used yoga to literally ohm their way to the top of their sport...you can do the same!

yoga is **the difference**

8

THE RECOVERY

1. **tree** (vrksasana)
2. **balancing superman** (virabhadrasana 3)
3. **seated forward bend** (paschimottanasana)

FROM THE MAT TO THE BOAT:
WHAT TO EXPECT FROM THESE POSES

▶ **feel the balance** in your body on the mat and learn what you need to do to maintain this balance and keep your weight even on your seat in the boat.

▶ **increase your sensory awareness** of what's around you while you're on the mat so you can feel the same connection with the water.

▶ Improves **posture and flexibility** so in the boat you maintain a strong, upright position leading forward and don't slouch over your oars.

▶ **strengthens** thighs, calves, ankles and spine so you can control your approach to the catch with your hamstrings until your shins are vertical.

the recovery

TREE

- *Stretches the muscles in your legs, especially in the thigh and groin, as well as the shoulders and chest.*

- *Improves balance by bringing awareness to your surroundings. If you can balance on the mat in this pose, you will have more control in the boat regardless of weather or race conditions.*

- *Strengthens thighs, ankles, calves and spine while improving their flexibility.*

HOW TO DO THIS POSE

1. STAND TALL
Feel your body get grounded, with your legs and feet supported against the floor. *Feel the same connection you do when pressing against the footboards. Keep the toes pressing down, stay connected.* Shift your weight slightly onto the left foot and bend your right knee. Reach down with your right hand and grab your right ankle lightly.

2. GET STRONG
Place the sole of your foot against the inner thigh (or wherever is comfortable). Be careful not to press against your knee. Keep your toes pointing to the floor.

Rest your hands on your hips. Pelvis is neutral: hip flexors pointing forward and tailbone scooped down. *Roll your shoulders down your back and relax, releasing all tension. Keep the left foot connected to the floor.*

3. BECOME AWARE
Press your hands together in front of your heart in a prayer position. Press your left foot into the floor and feel your right hip open. *Become aware of your surroundings. No disruptive movements. Concentrate on your breath and the very small adjustments you need to make within your musculature to remain balanced, like you would in the boat.*

4. BALANCE & BREATHE
Stay here 1 minute. If you're tired or your mind starts wandering, think about being technically precise rather than letting everything fall apart. *Just as if you're in the boat, keep your composure, grow a little taller in your spine, and remain relaxed.* Then release your right foot and step back to how you started, both feet on the floor. Repeat with your other leg.

PRECAUTIONS
If you suffer from headaches, insomnia, low or high blood pressure, or medical conditions that affect balance, take extra caution when raising your arms overhead. You can stand next to a wall if you need support.

think: balance

the recovery

BALANCING SUPERMAN

- *Strengthens the ankles, legs, shoulders and back muscles.*
- *Improves your balance and posture.*
- *Develops concentration and patience so you can have racelike intensity during practices.*
- *Improves your ability to keep your knees down coming up the slide so you don't lift them too early (before the hands and body are away), which causes the oar handle to lift up in the middle of the recovery.*

HOW TO DO THIS POSE

1. STAND TALL
Stand tall, exhale and step your left foot back into a high lunge. Your right knee should be close to a right angle. From this lunge position, stretch both arms up and overhead, parallel to each other. Exhale and lift your upper body tall.

2. GET FOCUSED
From this lunge position, bend at the waist, laying the midline of your torso down the midline of your right thigh. Stretch both arms forward, parallel to the floor and each other. Exhale, pressing your right heel into the ground. Straighten your front leg and lift your back leg slowly. At first, try lifting it only a few inches off the ground. *Like in the boat, your upper body plays a supporting role in the application of power. The legs are the star in the boat and doing this pose.*

3. IN CONTROL
The arms, torso and raised leg should be relatively parallel to the floor. Check to see that both hip joints are also parallel to the floor, facing downward. Energize your raised leg as it stretches out behind you. Energize your arms as they reach out in front of you. Raise your head.

4. BALANCE & BREATHE
Stay here for 30 seconds to 1 minute. *Focus on your breath to get you through this pose, making sure your exhale is longer than your inhale. As you exhale, like a pick drill, release all tension from your muscles.* Release your raised leg back into your lunge. Bring your hands to the floor on either side of your right foot. Bring your left foot forward to join your right. Return to a standing position. Repeat on the opposite side.

PRECAUTIONS
If you suffer from headaches, insomnia, low or high blood pressure, take caution and do the pose at the wall. You can face the wall and stretch your arms in front of you with your hands on the wall for extra support.

think: **balance**

the recovery

SEATED FORWARD BEND

- Quickly increases flexibility in your hamstrings and legs so you can keep your legs and knees down longer on the recovery.

- Calms the mind and directs your attention inward. This pose helps teach you to relax and find stillness even during a period of effort. You want to be just as calm and focused on the water, no stress or stiffness in your mind or muscles.

- Completely stretches your neck and spine.

HOW TO DO THIS POSE

1. SIT TALL
Sit on the floor with your legs straight in front of you. Feet should be flexed, with your toes pointing to the ceiling. Inhale deeply and raise your arms above your head, lengthening your spine. Lift up from the crown of your head. **Just as if you're in the boat, shoulders should be relaxed, low and away from your ears.**

2. LENGTHEN
Exhale as you bend your body forward from your hips, keeping your front torso and spine as long as possible. **This is like the "body over pause drill" - let the upper body pivot forward from the waist. It's the same as coming out of the finish - arms, then body away.** Stretch your hands out toward your feet. Grab the sides of your legs or feet, whichever is easier to reach.

3. RELAX
With each inhalation, lift and lengthen your torso slightly. With each exhalation, melt and relax a little more into the pose. Keep your neck and shoulders as relaxed as possible. **Your recovery will be smoother and the run on the boat substantially better because you will be able to execute quick hands away, then your body over - before bending your legs. You will have the flexibility you need to keep your knees down.**

4. BALANCE & BREATHE
Stay here for 1-3 minutes. Never force yourself into a forward bend. **Many rowers have tightness in their backs and legs, so your forward bends may not go very far forward when you start.** Exit this pose by lifting your torso away from your thighs, then slowly sit up.

PRECAUTIONS
If you suffer from chronic backaches or a slipped disc, consult your doctor first. One modification is to sit on a folded blanket and place a rolled up blanket under your knees in this pose. If pregnant, avoid this pose.

think: balance

RECOVERY NOTES

prepare
to succeed

**Perfection is not attainable,
but if we chase perfection we can catch excellence.**

Vince Lombardi

**Everyone has the desire to win,
but only champions have the desire to prepare.**

Author Unknown

on the mat

THE CATCH

1. **downward facing dog** (adho mukha svanasana)
2. **extended side angle** (utthita parsvakonasana)
3. **victory squat** (supta baddha konasana)

FROM THE MAT TO THE BOAT:
WHAT TO EXPECT FROM THESE POSES

▶ Strengthen your **core while increasing your calves' flexibility** so you can effortlessly get your seat forward without compromising your posture.

▶ Stretch your **arms straight and long** so in the boat you can fully extend them so your hands are outside the gunnels and you're able to maximize your stroke length without overextending your back or lunging.

▶ Learn what it feels like to **transfer your weight to your legs and feel balanced** so in the boat you can transfer your full body weight evenly onto the footboards, lift your hands, and push off with confidence.

in the boat

the catch

DOWNWARD FACING DOG

- *Targets specific sections of the body that are beneficial to rowers: shoulders, hands, spine, arches, hamstrings & calves.*
- *Builds strength in your arms and legs in particular. Hamstring and calf stretches like this help your legs so they won't become stiff or strained due to the constant bending and straightening while rowing.*
- *Calms the mind.*

HOW TO DO THIS POSE

1. PREPARATION
Begin on the floor on your hands and knees, as if imitating a table. Spread your palms and fingers wide, and curl your toes under. Exhale and lift your knees away from the floor. Keep the knees slightly bent and the heels lifted off the floor at first. As you straighten your arms, press your hands firmly into the floor.

2. GET FLEXIBLE
Stretch your heels down to the floor. *Your goal is to get your feet flat on the floor like they would be at the catch against the footboards.* This will happen in time as you become more flexible. Straighten your knees but don't lock them. Lift your hips high so your buttocks points up to the ceiling. Your body is in an inverted "V" shape.

3. FEEL CONNECTED
As your hands and arms press into the ground, draw your shoulder blades down toward your tailbone. Lengthen your spine. Keep your head between your arms, don't let it hang. *You are pressing with your hands and pushing with your feet to get length in both halves of your body.*

4. BALANCE & BREATHE
Stay here for 1-3 minutes. *Just as you focus your mind on getting the most out of every stroke, focus on this pose. Concentrate on your breath and stretching your calves so their flexibility increases and you can get your seat forward to the catch without compromising your posture.* When you're ready to exit, bend your knees to the floor, then your elbows.

PRECAUTIONS
If you suffer from carpel tunnel syndrome, high blood pressure, headaches, or have a chronic back injury, consult your physician. Do not do this pose if you are in the last trimester of a pregnancy.

think: connection

the catch

EXTENDED SIDE ANGLE

- Stretches the sides of the body, particularly the waist and ribcage. This allows for more rotation at the catch and a longer stroke.
- Strengthens and increases the flexibility of the hips, legs and ankles.
- Opens the chest and increases your lung capacity.
- Muscles in the shoulders, neck and arms are toned and stretched.

HOW TO DO THIS POSE

1. PREPARATION
From standing, step your feet 3-4 feet apart. Raise your arms parallel to the floor and reach out to the sides, palms facing down. Turn your left foot in slightly to the right and your right foot out to the right 90 degrees. Line up the right heel with the middle of the left foot. Bend your right knee so it's over your right ankle and your shin is perpendicular to the floor. Try to bring the right thigh parallel to the floor.

2. GET LONG
Exhale, focus and bend your torso to the right, keeping the palm of your right hand on the floor outside you. Your left leg is straight. Reach your left arm up toward the ceiling and stretch from your left heel through to your left fingertips. Lengthen the entire left side of your body. *If you're a port rower, this will lengthen your stroke. When you repeat this pose on the other side, it will lengthen your starboard stroke.*

3. EXTEND & STRETCH
Find your center of gravity and try to center your weight between your feet as much as possible. *Just like in the boat, stay on your legs, keep your weight low.* Your spine should be straight, and your head, shoulders and hips are in a line. If it's difficult to place your palm on the floor, touch your fingertips to the floor or rest your elbow on your front thigh with your forearm.

4. BALANCE & BREATHE
Commit to this pose for 30 seconds to 1 minute. *Extend your arms, stretching them a little farther away from you with each exhalation. You're aiming to increase the length of your stroke at the catch.* To exit, press the right foot into the floor, lift your right palm off the floor and straighten your right leg. Return to standing and repeat on the other side.

PRECAUTIONS
If you suffer from headaches, insomnia, low or high blood pressure, take extra caution. If you have any type of neck problems, do not look up. Instead, look either straight ahead or down at the floor.

think: connection

the catch

VICTORY SQUAT

- Opens your chest and hips.
- Strengthens the lower body and core quickly.
- Increases your calves' flexibility and your overall posture so you don't slouch at the catch and cause soreness in your neck and back.
- Improves boat set as you learn to press with your feet equally into the ground, just as you keep your feet flat and connected to the foot stretchers.

HOW TO DO THIS POSE

1. MOVE MINDFULLY

From standing, turn each foot out 45 degrees. Bend your knees and lower your hips and body to the ground so you are in a squat. *This movement is like coming up the slide to the catch, so move slowly. Your shins should be vertical. Keep your shoulders level and relaxed. No shoulder shrugging - on the mat or in the boat!*

2. THINK POSTURE

When you are lowered to the floor, make sure your knees remain behind your toes and try not to lean forward or hunch. Your chest should be up. *Get long in your spine and straighten your back - don't compromise your core and back support. Although your knees are apart in this pose, this IS your catch position.*

3. IN CONTROL

Bend your elbows so your palms are in a prayer position in front of your heart. Keep your elbows below your shoulders. Keep your weight evenly distributed on each foot, with your weight centered between them. *Gaze at a fixed point in front of you, the same way you key in on the rower in front of you or down the stern of the boat.*

4. BALANCE & BREATHE

Stay here for 1 minute. *Make sure to concentrate on your breath and keeping your core strong and your back as straight and tall as possible. Remember your coach's call: Keep your weight on your feet. Visualize being at the catch, coiled up and ready to push off without hesitation.* Release the pose and return to stand.

PRECAUTIONS

If you suffer from headaches, insomnia, low or high blood pressure, or if you have had a recent or chronic injury to the legs, hips, back or shoulders take extra caution in this position.

think: connection

CATCH NOTES

believe in yourself

Always dream and shoot higher than you know you can do. Don't bother to be better than your contemporaries or predecessors. Try to be better than yourself.

William Faulkner

Confidence is contagious. So is lack of confidence.

Vince Lombardi

28

on the mat

THE DRIVE

1. **warrior** (virabhadrasana)
2. **bridge** (setu bandha sarvangasana)
3. **chair** (utkatasana)

FROM THE MAT TO THE BOAT:
WHAT TO EXPECT FROM THESE POSES

▶ Develop a sense of **linking legs, back and arms** so these 3 muscle groups carry the oars through the water at a constant speed, with the control to keep your arms loose and allowing your legs to lead the drive.

▶ Strengthen your glutes and legs to develop **explosive leg power**.

▶ Connect to your core so you have firm **upper body posture**.

▶ Improve **flexibility in your legs and knees** so in the boat you can easily keep them flat through to the finish.

in the boat

the drive

WARRIOR

- Will make your legs strong and improve your balance while stretching your thighs, calves and ankles.
- Develops equal strength and stability in your legs.
- Strengthens shoulders, arms and the back muscles.
- Improves the flexibility in your legs and knees so you're able to keep your knees down during the drive, and through to the finish.

HOW TO DO THIS POSE

1. STAND TALL
From a standing position, move your right foot about 4 feet away from your left foot, so they are hip width apart with your toes pointed forward. Raise your arms perpendicular to the floor and reach toward the ceiling. Lift from your lower back to get taller. Turn your left foot in slightly and rotate your right foot out 90 degrees to the right - so the right heel intersects with the left heel.

2. GET ALIGNED
Exhale and rotate your torso to the right, squaring off your pelvis and hip flexors with the front of your mat. Imagine each hipbone as a car headlight that you want facing forward. Bend your right leg slightly so your right knee is over your right ankle and the shin is perpendicular to the floor. Your left leg is straight. Your weight is evenly distributed between each foot. Breathe.

3. IN CONTROL
As you settle into this pose, reach up confidently with your arms as if you're hanging on the oar. Keep your shoulders relaxed and down. You can either look straight ahead or you can tilt your head back and look up at your hands. *Release all tension - it affects your balance in this pose and the set in the boat.*

4. BALANCE & BREATHE
Stay here for 30 seconds to 1 minute. *Like in the boat, your legs are extremely powerful in this pose. Don't abandon your technique for power - continue reaching up and getting long.* Release the pose by exhaling as you bring your arms back down to your sides. Step back to the original standing pose. Take a few breaths, then repeat on the other side.

PRECAUTIONS
If you suffer from high blood pressure or heart problems, take extra caution in this position. If you have any neck problems, do not look up at your hands, instead look straight ahead.

think: power

the **drive**

BRIDGE

- Stretches the chest, neck and spine while opening the heart and lungs.
- Rejuvenates tired legs.
- Strengthens your glutes and legs for explosive power in the boat.

HOW TO DO THIS POSE

1. PREPARATION
Lie on your back, with your hands and arms at either side. Bend your knees and place your feet on the floor, with your heels close to your buttocks. Your feet should be about 6 inches apart.

2. GET BALANCED
Place your hands under your back, with your palms supporting your hips. Exhale and focus, gently raising your hips as you press your feet into the floor. Lift your buttocks until your thighs are about parallel to the floor. Keep your knees over your heels and feel your spine lengthen. At this point, release your hands and support yourself with your elbows on the floor.

3. FEEL CONNECTED
Connect to your breath and take a few long, slow, deep breaths while you hold this pose. Calm your mind, let your back loosen, and keep your feet grounded into the floor. *Imagine a pick drill: hands are relaxed, shoulders aren't tense, legs loose. Tune into your body and identify where you hold onto any unnecessary tension. Release it on the mat, so you can release it in the boat.*

4. BALANCE & BREATHE
Stay here for 30 seconds to 1 minute. Practice patience, you can do this pose. *As you lift your midsection, connect to your core so your posture in the boat improves and you can maintain a straight back and swing effortlessly.* To exit, exhale and roll your spine slowly back onto the floor. Release your arms.

PRECAUTIONS
Avoid this pose if you have any neck problems or have experienced a neck or spinal injury. If you have any problems with your knees, use caution as this pose places stress on your knees. Not advised for the last trimester of a pregnancy.

think: power

the drive

CHAIR

- Powers up your lower body, strengthening your legs and lower back.
- Stretches your shoulders and opens the chest.
- Improves your sense of balance.
- Links your arm, back and leg muscles so you know what it feels like to engage all 3, just as they work together to carry the oar through the water at a constant speed.

HOW TO DO THIS POSE

1. STAND TALL

Stand tall as you inhale deeply. Raise your arms above you so they are shoulder width apart, parallel, and palms facing each other. **Your shoulders should be low just like when you row, make sure they're not up by your ears. Your arms should be relaxed and loose.** Feel the extension and stretch in your arms.l.

2. IN CONTROL

Exhale as you bend your knees. Imagine you're going to sit in a chair. The goal is to take your thighs as close to parallel to the floor as possible. Your hips shouldn't go below your knees. Your heels stay on the floor. Keep your back straight. At any point in this pose, you should be able to see your toes.

3. POWER UP YOUR LEGS

Engage your legs - they should feel strong and stable. Your inner thighs should be parallel to each other. **Keep your arms long, loose and strong - but relaxed, as if you're hanging on the oar. Let your legs carry the weight and support you, just like during the drive. Both feet press equally into the ground, just like the foot stretchers.**

4. BALANCE & BREATHE

Stay here for 30 seconds to 1 minute, very relaxed. **Pretend you're in the boat: eyes up, chin up.** Focus on your breathing and relax any tension in your body. Melt your shoulder blades down your back. To exit this pose, just straighten your legs as you exhale. Release your arms down to your sides and return to the original standing pose.

PRECAUTIONS

If you suffer from headaches, insomnia, low or high blood pressure, take extra caution. In case of recent injury to the knees, this pose is better to be avoided. If you have recent or chronic injury to the hips avoid this pose.

think: power

DRIVE NOTES

practice
with racelike
intensity

Most people never run far enough on their first wind to find out they've got a second.

William James

Hard training, easy combat. Easy training, hard combat.

Marshall Suvorov, Russian General

on the mat

THE FINISH

1. **side plank** (vasisthasana)
2. **upward plank** (purvottanasana)
3. **full boat** (paripurna navasana)

FROM THE MAT TO THE BOAT:
WHAT TO EXPECT FROM THESE POSES

▶ **strengthen your core and maximize your stroke length** by keeping your chest open in the boat as you lay back, your elbows drawn behind you and shoulder blades squeezed together without strain on your lower back.

▶ Learn to **release tension from your body and mind** so you're able to quickly follow through with your arms and make a smooth transition from the drive to a controlled approach back up the slide to the catch.

▶ **develop your body posture** so in the boat you're able to keep your head up, legs flat and maintain the connection between your feet and footboards.

in the boat

the finish

SIDE PLANK

- Quickly strengthens your arms, shoulders, wrists and legs while toning the lower back.

- Stretches the backs of the legs so you're able to keep your legs flat and your knees down in the boat on the finish and as you come up the slide on the recovery.

- Improves your overall sense of balance and control.

HOW TO DO THIS POSE

1. PREPARE
Lay on your stomach with your hands flat on the floor on either side of your shoulders, fingers pointing forward. Curl your toes under. Push yourself up with your arms, as if you were doing a push up. Keep your shoulder blades firmly against your back, with a long straight spine. You want your shoulders directly over your wrists. Engage your core to keep your body in this plank position.

2. GET STRONG
Shift your body so you are balancing on the outside edge of your left foot. Stack your right foot on top of your left. Move your right hand onto your right hip, rotating your torso to the right at the same time. You are now supporting your weight on 2 points: your outer left foot and your left hand.

3. IN CONTROL
Your body is in one long diagonal line. You can keep your right hand on your hip or you can stretch it up toward the ceiling. *Your shoulders should be completely relaxed. Use your core and upper body strength to balance in this pose, keeping your upper body very still, just as you would at the finish in the boat.*

4. BALANCE & BREATHE
Commit to this pose for 15-30 seconds, pressing your heels toward the floor for support. *If it helps, be your own coxswain: give yourself a Focus 20 and count to yourself to hold the pose.* To release, flip back to the plank position and repeat on the right side. When the right side is finished, slowly lower your body back to the ground so you are laying flat on your stomach again.

PRECAUTIONS
If you suffer from a serious shoulder, elbow, ankle or wrist injury, avoid this pose until healed. In case of a chronic or recent arm or shoulder injury, avoid this pose.

think: **control**

the finish

UPWARD PLANK

- Stretches your shoulders, opens the chest, develops your core, and loosens the front of your ankles.

- Targets concentration and hones your ability to focus.

- Strengthens your arms, wrists and legs.

- Dramatically lowers stress levels. In the boat it's important to control stress levels, especially during a race, so you won't grip the oar handles too tightly and you're able to keep your arms loose so your legs power the boat.

HOW TO DO THIS POSE

1. PREPARE
Sit with your legs out straight in front of you. **Keep your knees down like they would be in the boat and visualize being in the finish position.** Place your hands a few inches behind your hips with your fingers pointing toward your toes. Bend your knees and place your feet flat on the floor.

2. GET STRONG
Exhale and focus, pressing your feet and hands against the ground. Lift your hips up to the ceiling untiil you come into what looks like a reverse table pos: your torso and thighs are almost parallel to the floor. Check to see that your arms and shins are aproximately perpendicular to the floor as well.

3. CORE CONTROL
Straighten your legs one at a time. Keep your hips lifted high. Engage your shoulder blades so they are able to support the lift in your chest. Keep your core strong and engaged so your body is in a long line. Mindfully, and it feels good to you, slowly release and drop your head back. Relax.

4. BALANCE & BREATHE
Stay here for 30 seconds. **Release your mind and find your balance. All muscles are relaxed and loose, with no tension or gripping anywhere - just as they should be in the boat.** To release this pose, lower your hips and sit down as you exhale slowly.

PRECAUTIONS
If you suffer from a wrist or neck injury, practice caution when doing this pose. For a neck injury, you can support your head against a wall for increased support and stability.

think: **control**

the finish

FULL BOAT

- Effectively targets your abdomen, hip flexors, lower back and spine.

- Is a powerhouse! Your core will quickly become more powerful and agile so that it can support and maintain your layback at the finish in addition to allowing for a controlled swing forward into the recovery.

- This pose also relieves stress and improves concentration.

HOW TO DO THIS POSE

1. POSTURE
Sit on the floor with your legs out straight in front of you. Place your hands behind your hips with your fingers pointing forward on the floor. Lift from your lower spine, sitting tall as you lean back slightly. Resist the urge to round your back. Instead, keep your back straight as you sit and balance on your two sitting bones and tailbone.

2. PREPARATION
Breathe deeply and bend your knees, lifting your feet off the floor. If possible, slowly start to straighten your knees and lift your legs so your toes are slightly above your eyes. Try to get your legs angled at 45 degrees from the floor, so your body is in a V-position. If this is too difficult in the beginning, you can keep your knees bent and your shins parallel to the floor.

3. CORE CONTROL
Reach your arms out alongside your legs, keeping them parallel to the floor and to each other. Or for more support, you can either keep your hands on the floor next to your hips or you can hold onto the backs of your thighs. *Just as in the boat, keep your spine as straight as possible. Relax and drop your shoulders. Eyes forward.* Breathe deeply.

4. BALANCE & BREATHE
Stay here for 10-20 seconds when you first begin. As your core strength increases, you will be able to remain in here for 1 minute or more. *Like in the boat, long arms, long legs. With each exhale, open your chest a little more and lay back, feeling the stability coming from your core strength and a straight back.* To exit, release your legs as you exhale, sit upright as you inhale.

PRECAUTIONS
If you suffer from headaches, insomnia, low or high blood pressure, heart problems, have either an abdominal or tailbone injury, or are pregnant, take extra caution in this position. If you have a neck injury, sit with your back near a wall so you're resting the back of your head on the wall.

think: **control**

FINISH NOTES

control **the breath**
control **the mind**

Reject your sense of inury and the injury itself disappears.

Marcus Aurelius

Pain is temporary. It may last a minute, or an hour, or a day, or a year, but eventually it will subside and something else will take its place. If I quit, however, it lasts forever.

Lance Armstrong

The fact that you bought this book means you're interested in stepping up your training. Whether you want to improve your balance, concentration, reduce your risk for injury so you can train harder, or if you're competing for FISA Worlds and looking for whatever advantage you can, this book has the answers and will help.

This book comes with a warning: if you follow the instructions and suggested training schedule, you WILL experience results and you WILL become a better rower. *Yoga for Rowers* works! In order to experience the maximum benefit the program has to offer, you need to make a personal commitment for one month. The initial month is critical. The first two weeks will be the most challenging as you will be trying new poses and stretching your muscles in ways you might not have done before. Stick with it. Connect with your breath and know while you may compete in the boat and seat race, when you're practicing yoga there's no such thing as mat racing. Whatever you're able to do is exactly where you should be - it's the exact opposite of rowing in a sense. Instead of pushing yourself harder, when you're on the mat just relax, breathe and be patient. So for all you alpha personalities out there who want to smash the 1:24.1 indoor world record split time set in 2007, I can't stress this enough: TAKE IT SLOW. BE PATIENT WITH YOURSELF. This might be the most challenging part: quieting your mind. You won't master these poses your first time on the mat, but if you dedicate 3-4 days a week to this program, after one month, you will look forward to them. They'll be easier, you'll see a difference on the erg and in the boat, and most importantly, the poses will become a habit.

Your rowing will improve only as much as you commit to this program.

What happens after Month 1? This program will be part of your life. It's not difficult to find time to practice because yoga doesn't require an enormous time commitment. While it's recommended to dedicate the time soley for yoga - preferably in a space without distractions - life doesn't always cooperate and we need to squeeze a pose or two in when we can even though we're tethered to our Blackberrys. Some suggestions:

- Practice before/after erging, rowing or your regular workout.
- Practice when you wake up in the morning. As your coffee is brewing or you're watching the morning news, sneak in 10 minutes to do the poses in 1 or 2 of the stroke sections.
- During lunch, practice tree for a minute.
- Before bed or while watching tv, wind down in your favorite poses.

The best news is the more frequently you practice yoga, the better your rowing will become! There is NO LIMIT to your potential!

prepare to succeed

Ways to Use this Book:

Stroke Cycle
Perform each of the 3 poses in all 4 phases, moving through the entire stroke cycle 3 times. Select the 1st pose from the Recovery section, the 1st pose from the Catch, 1st pose from the Drive, and 1st pose from the Finish. Then move onto the 2nd pose in each section, followed by the 3rd pose until all poses have been performed one time.

Pinpoint
After performing all 12 poses, assess which poses are challenging to you. Write them down here:

_____   _____

_____   _____

_____   _____

_____

* Make certain to incorporate these poses several times each week. Either as a cool down from your workout, or as an easy secondary workout for the day.

Focused
As your strength and balance improve, work an entire section (with no breaks) 3-5 times allowing 1 minute between cycles. For example, select the Catch section and perform Downward Facing Dog, Extended Side Angle and Victory Squat 3-5 times, with 1 minute rest between reps. This routine will allow the muscles to be worked harder while also allowing the muscles to lengthen.

Recovery
After a particularly hard workout on the erg or water (immediately or a few hours later), focus on poses that lengthen your muscles, strengthen your back, move energy from your core to your extremities, and stimulate blood flow - this will help promote a faster recovery. Select from the following

poses and do each one 3-4 times, resting 2-3 minutes between cycles: Downward Dog, Extended Side Angle, Seated Forward Bend, Warrior and Side Plank.

Consistency

Since this is a lifelong pursuit, to help keep you on track after your first month, there are four weekly calendars on the following pages with all 12 poses listed for each day. These are designed to insure your practices are complete. At the end of the day or before you go to bed, check off the poses you did that day. Be honest, no cheating! If you didn't do any yoga or you rested that day, leave the day blank or put a big "X" through it. Make sure to do all 12 poses 3-4 times each week. We all have a bad habit of estimating in our minds just how much we've worked out - and usually our estimates are way off. At the end of the week, you will be able to look at these calendars and see EXACTLY what you did and/or did not do. You will have improved if you practiced!

prepare to succeed

YOGA for ROWERS
WORKOUTS:

week one

	SUNDAY	MONDAY	TUESDAY
RECOVERY	☐ Tree ☐ Superman ☐ Plank	☐ Tree ☐ Superman ☐ Plank	☐ Tree ☐ Superman ☐ Plank
CATCH	☐ Down Dog ☐ Ext. Angle ☐ V. Squat	☐ Down Dog ☐ Ext. Angle ☐ V. Squat	☐ Down Dog ☐ Ext. Angle ☐ V. Squat
DRIVE	☐ Warrior ☐ Chair ☐ Bridge	☐ Warrior ☐ Chair ☐ Bridge	☐ Warrior ☐ Chair ☐ Bridge
FINISH	☐ Side Plank ☐ Up Plank ☐ Full Boat	☐ Side Plank ☐ Up Plank ☐ Full Boat	☐ Side Plank ☐ Up Plank ☐ Full Boat

Poses that are challenging and require special attention:

_____   _____

_____   _____

For maximum impact, aim for 3-4 practices each week. Check off the pose(s) you've done each day, aiming for all 12 poses. By checking off the poses, at the completion of

PREPARE TO SUCCEED

WEDNESDAY	THURSDAY	FRIDAY	SATURDAY
RECOVERY ☐ Tree ☐ Superman ☐ Plank	**RECOVERY** ☐ Tree ☐ Superman ☐ Plank	**RECOVERY** ☐ Tree ☐ Superman ☐ Plank	**RECOVERY** ☐ Tree ☐ Superman ☐ Plank
CATCH ☐ Down Dog ☐ Ext. Angle ☐ V. Squat	**CATCH** ☐ Down Dog ☐ Ext. Angle ☐ V. Squat	**CATCH** ☐ Down Dog ☐ Ext. Angle ☐ V. Squat	**CATCH** ☐ Down Dog ☐ Ext. Angle ☐ V. Squat
DRIVE ☐ Warrior ☐ Chair ☐ Bridge	**DRIVE** ☐ Warrior ☐ Chair ☐ Bridge	**DRIVE** ☐ Warrior ☐ Chair ☐ Bridge	**DRIVE** ☐ Warrior ☐ Chair ☐ Bridge
FINISH ☐ Side Plank ☐ Up Plank ☐ Full Boat	**FINISH** ☐ Side Plank ☐ Up Plank ☐ Full Boat	**FINISH** ☐ Side Plank ☐ Up Plank ☐ Full Boat	**FINISH** ☐ Side Plank ☐ Up Plank ☐ Full Boat

WEEK 1 RESULTS
notes

the month you will see exactly how much effort you committed to this program. Give the program one month and you WILL see results!

YOGA for ROWERS WORKOUTS:

week two

	SUNDAY	MONDAY	TUESDAY
	RECOVERY ☐ Tree ☐ Superman ☐ Plank	**RECOVERY** ☐ Tree ☐ Superman ☐ Plank	**RECOVERY** ☐ Tree ☐ Superman ☐ Plank
	CATCH ☐ Down Dog ☐ Ext. Angle ☐ V. Squat	**CATCH** ☐ Down Dog ☐ Ext. Angle ☐ V. Squat	**CATCH** ☐ Down Dog ☐ Ext. Angle ☐ V. Squat
	DRIVE ☐ Warrior ☐ Chair ☐ Bridge	**DRIVE** ☐ Warrior ☐ Chair ☐ Bridge	**DRIVE** ☐ Warrior ☐ Chair ☐ Bridge
	FINISH ☐ Side Plank ☐ Up Plank ☐ Full Boat	**FINISH** ☐ Side Plank ☐ Up Plank ☐ Full Boat	**FINISH** ☐ Side Plank ☐ Up Plank ☐ Full Boat

Poses that are challenging and require special attention:

_____   _____

_____   _____

For maximum impact, aim for 3-4 practices each week. Check off the pose(s) you've done each day, aiming for all 12 poses. By checking off the poses, at the completion of

PREPARE TO SUCCEED

WEDNESDAY	THURSDAY	FRIDAY	SATURDAY
RECOVERY ☐ Tree ☐ Superman ☐ Plank	**RECOVERY** ☐ Tree ☐ Superman ☐ Plank	**RECOVERY** ☐ Tree ☐ Superman ☐ Plank	**RECOVERY** ☐ Tree ☐ Superman ☐ Plank
CATCH ☐ Down Dog ☐ Ext. Angle ☐ V. Squat	**CATCH** ☐ Down Dog ☐ Ext. Angle ☐ V. Squat	**CATCH** ☐ Down Dog ☐ Ext. Angle ☐ V. Squat	**CATCH** ☐ Down Dog ☐ Ext. Angle ☐ V. Squat
DRIVE ☐ Warrior ☐ Chair ☐ Bridge	**DRIVE** ☐ Warrior ☐ Chair ☐ Bridge	**DRIVE** ☐ Warrior ☐ Chair ☐ Bridge	**DRIVE** ☐ Warrior ☐ Chair ☐ Bridge
FINISH ☐ Side Plank ☐ Up Plank ☐ Full Boat	**FINISH** ☐ Side Plank ☐ Up Plank ☐ Full Boat	**FINISH** ☐ Side Plank ☐ Up Plank ☐ Full Boat	**FINISH** ☐ Side Plank ☐ Up Plank ☐ Full Boat

WEEK 2 RESULTS notes

the month you will see exactly how much effort you committed to this program. Give the program one month and you WILL see results!

YOGA for ROWERS WORKOUTS:

week three

	SUNDAY	MONDAY	TUESDAY
RECOVERY	☐ Tree ☐ Superman ☐ Plank	☐ Tree ☐ Superman ☐ Plank	☐ Tree ☐ Superman ☐ Plank
CATCH	☐ Down Dog ☐ Ext. Angle ☐ V. Squat	☐ Down Dog ☐ Ext. Angle ☐ V. Squat	☐ Down Dog ☐ Ext. Angle ☐ V. Squat
DRIVE	☐ Warrior ☐ Chair ☐ Bridge	☐ Warrior ☐ Chair ☐ Bridge	☐ Warrior ☐ Chair ☐ Bridge
FINISH	☐ Side Plank ☐ Up Plank ☐ Full Boat	☐ Side Plank ☐ Up Plank ☐ Full Boat	☐ Side Plank ☐ Up Plank ☐ Full Boat

Poses that are challenging and require special attention:

_____   _____

_____   _____

For maximum impact, aim for 3-4 practices each week. Check off the pose(s) you've done each day, aiming for all 12 poses. By checking off the poses, at the completion of

PREPARE TO SUCCEED

WEDNESDAY	THURSDAY	FRIDAY	SATURDAY
RECOVERY ☐ Tree ☐ Superman ☐ Plank	**RECOVERY** ☐ Tree ☐ Superman ☐ Plank	**RECOVERY** ☐ Tree ☐ Superman ☐ Plank	**RECOVERY** ☐ Tree ☐ Superman ☐ Plank
CATCH ☐ Down Dog ☐ Ext. Angle ☐ V. Squat	**CATCH** ☐ Down Dog ☐ Ext. Angle ☐ V. Squat	**CATCH** ☐ Down Dog ☐ Ext. Angle ☐ V. Squat	**CATCH** ☐ Down Dog ☐ Ext. Angle ☐ V. Squat
DRIVE ☐ Warrior ☐ Chair ☐ Bridge	**DRIVE** ☐ Warrior ☐ Chair ☐ Bridge	**DRIVE** ☐ Warrior ☐ Chair ☐ Bridge	**DRIVE** ☐ Warrior ☐ Chair ☐ Bridge
FINISH ☐ Side Plank ☐ Up Plank ☐ Full Boat	**FINISH** ☐ Side Plank ☐ Up Plank ☐ Full Boat	**FINISH** ☐ Side Plank ☐ Up Plank ☐ Full Boat	**FINISH** ☐ Side Plank ☐ Up Plank ☐ Full Boat

WEEK 3
RESULTS
notes

the month you will see exactly how much effort you committed to this program. Give the program one month and you WILL see results!

YOGA for ROWERS WORKOUTS:

week four

	SUNDAY	MONDAY	TUESDAY
	RECOVERY ☐ Tree ☐ Superman ☐ Plank	**RECOVERY** ☐ Tree ☐ Superman ☐ Plank	**RECOVERY** ☐ Tree ☐ Superman ☐ Plank
	CATCH ☐ Down Dog ☐ Ext. Angle ☐ V. Squat	**CATCH** ☐ Down Dog ☐ Ext. Angle ☐ V. Squat	**CATCH** ☐ Down Dog ☐ Ext. Angle ☐ V. Squat
	DRIVE ☐ Warrior ☐ Chair ☐ Bridge	**DRIVE** ☐ Warrior ☐ Chair ☐ Bridge	**DRIVE** ☐ Warrior ☐ Chair ☐ Bridge
	FINISH ☐ Side Plank ☐ Up Plank ☐ Full Boat	**FINISH** ☐ Side Plank ☐ Up Plank ☐ Full Boat	**FINISH** ☐ Side Plank ☐ Up Plank ☐ Full Boat

Poses that are challenging and require special attention:

_____   _____

_____   _____

For maximum impact, aim for 3-4 practices each week. Check off the pose(s) you've done each day, aiming for all 12 poses. By checking off the poses, at the completion of

PREPARE TO SUCCEED

WEDNESDAY	THURSDAY	FRIDAY	SATURDAY
RECOVERY ☐ Tree ☐ Superman ☐ Plank	**RECOVERY** ☐ Tree ☐ Superman ☐ Plank	**RECOVERY** ☐ Tree ☐ Superman ☐ Plank	**RECOVERY** ☐ Tree ☐ Superman ☐ Plank
CATCH ☐ Down Dog ☐ Ext. Angle ☐ V. Squat	**CATCH** ☐ Down Dog ☐ Ext. Angle ☐ V. Squat	**CATCH** ☐ Down Dog ☐ Ext. Angle ☐ V. Squat	**CATCH** ☐ Down Dog ☐ Ext. Angle ☐ V. Squat
DRIVE ☐ Warrior ☐ Chair ☐ Bridge	**DRIVE** ☐ Warrior ☐ Chair ☐ Bridge	**DRIVE** ☐ Warrior ☐ Chair ☐ Bridge	**DRIVE** ☐ Warrior ☐ Chair ☐ Bridge
FINISH ☐ Side Plank ☐ Up Plank ☐ Full Boat	**FINISH** ☐ Side Plank ☐ Up Plank ☐ Full Boat	**FINISH** ☐ Side Plank ☐ Up Plank ☐ Full Boat	**FINISH** ☐ Side Plank ☐ Up Plank ☐ Full Boat

WEEK 4
RESULTS
notes

the month you will see exactly how much effort you committed to this program. Give the program one month and you WILL see results!

Taking it from the mat to the boat.

That's what this book is all about after all. You're already training hard, either on your own or with a coach. This book is meant to augment your current regime by teaching you an easy-to-follow yoga practice that will translate into real results in the boat. These 12 poses will elevate your oarsmanship exponentially: Increasing your **length of stroke**. Improving your **power**. Allowing you to train harder with fewer injuries so you maximize your **stroke rate**. Developing the sensory awareness, balance and control which are mandatory for clean finishes - and for eliminating drag by keeping your blades off the water on the recovery. Practicing yoga and thereby fine tuning these important skills is that extra step your competitors aren't taking which gives you a definite advantage on race day.

There's a quote I believe that can be related to taking those first important steps to learning yoga one pose at a time and applying them to your rowing:

"Do today what others will not, so that you may do tomorrow what others cannot."

There are so many physically gifted and talented athletes, but few of them achieve their potential, let alone their personal goals. The mental side of their game is what makes all the difference. Ask yourself, how do YOU handle stress at a regatta? When the wind is high, waves crashing inside the shell, maybe there's snow - do your muscles involuntarily tense and negatively affect your technique? How does your body tolerate pain in the last 1,000 meters of a head race? What is your brain telling you during a close race - is your will strong and positive enough so you're able to focus on the task at hand and pull off a win, or does your mind play tricks and mentally you fold? The ability to shut off the noise between your ears is invaluable. Shoot the hamster on the wheel! This yoga program teaches this.

After reading this book you will find yoga promotes flexibility, strength and mental discipline. After the first week of doing the yoga program outlined in this book, your mental game will be sharpened. Your mind will be filled with positive affirmations and your overall stress and tension levels will be dramatically lowered. By week two, your muscles and joints will begin to

ohm your way to gold!

be looser and more pliable. And the longer you practice the poses on the mat, your training will take on a renewed vibrancy as you're able to focus on your strokes and application of power with fewer injuries and a faster recovery time.

BY READING THIS BOOK

Build Internal Awareness + Boat Awareness

⬇

You want to achieve a total synchronicity of your mind, muscles and the boat. The more you practice yoga and take it's lessons with you onto the water, the less and less distinction there will be between these 3.

Yoga will also help you dominate on race day! When you're racing and your legs are burning, lungs about to explode, your coxie's shouting something unintelligible and your arms feel more like jello than rope - yoga will bring you back to your center. You will have perfected the connection between body and mind. Consciously inhaling and exhaling will effectively block out the pain. Your mental game will keep you focused and positive, a sense of inner calm prevails. You are intently focused on a single goal without distraction - getting across the finish line first while moving at maximum power with precise posture and technique. By falling back on the lessons you learned on the mat, external factors will become nonexistent. Your ability to focus on each stroke and what you personally need to do to move the boat better will be unparalleled. Without realizing it, the race will almost seem easy to you.

And when the season is over and your competition is left in your wake, you can look at your medals and know you earned them because you took your training to a whole new level, both mentally and physically.

Yeah. Yoga is pretty powerful stuff. It's GOLDEN to be zen!

I hope you enjoy this book and the training it provides. I know you will become a better rower because of these yoga poses.

Wishing you the very best of success with your season!

Carye

ohm your way to gold!

about the author:

The Yoda Coxswain: Part Sun Tzu, part yogi - Chrys brings mental focus and energy to her boats. VP of Marketing for Scratch Off Works, a niche printing company specializing in printed and online scratch off games, promotions and fundraisers for companies around the globe. Morning Ritual: Back-to-back power yoga classes or a 5am row on the Cuyahoga, followed by a Starbucks cappucino or wheatgrass shot. Her Uniform: Color coordinated JL Racing spandex at the boathouse, D&G skirts and stilettos at the office. Likes to cook and loves to travel. Favorite Books: Steve Martin's *Picasso at the Lapin Agile* and *The Fountainhead* by Ayn Rand. Reading List: *The Economist*, *NY Times*. Self-proclaimed iPod junkie.

After spending 10 years watching her brother Jim bring home medals, she decided to join the sport too as a sculler and coxswain, and hasn't looked back since! Through the Western Reserve Rowing Association, Chrys has rowed, coxed and medaled in several regional regattas, including the Head of the Charles, Head of the Ohio and Head of the Cuyahoga. She serves on the board for Western Reserve Rowing Association. She is webmaster of www.YogaForRowers.com and the author of *Yoga For Rowers*, a book that's first of it's kind illustrating the benefits of yoga - mental focus, strength, power and flexibility - as they apply to competitive rowing.

Head of the Charles 2009: Club Fours Men Category.
Charlie Gritzmacher (3), Paul Kopp (bow), Bill Rickman (stroke), Chrys Kozak (cox), Gavin Farrell (2).